Drawing in the Dark
The Art of Sol Schwartz
Norman Rockwell Museum

This book is dedicated to my wife
Elayne Polly Bernstein Schwartz.

A visionary who has devoted her life to
making this a better world for all of us.

For Joel and Joan,
with much love,
Sid Schwartz

Sol Schwartz: Drawing in the Dark

The spirit of music and movement are captured in the art of Sol Schwartz, whose vibrant, spontaneous drawings have reflected the beauty and excitement of music, theater, and dance, in the Berkshires and beyond, for more than a decade.

As the curtain rises and the lights go down, the energy and emotion of live performance provides a swell of inspiration for Schwartz's work. Created on location from his place in the audience at Tanglewood Music Center, Shakespeare & Company, Barrington Stage Company, and Jacob's Pillow, his artworks reflect the intensity and focus of his gifted subjects, providing a unique window into their experience.

"It happened by accident," the artist said. "I used to make little sketches in the corners of my programs when I attended concerts." Eventually, he began bringing a sketchbook along to work in, and over the years, has completed thousands of studies, including likenesses of such musical, dance, and theater superstars as Andre Previn, Itzak Perlman, Emanuel Ax, Seiji Ozawa, Yo-Yo Ma, Katherine Dunham, Savion Glover, Mark Morris, Tina Packer, and many others. "The novelty of my work is that I do it while a performance is underway, sometimes in the pitch dark," Schwartz notes. He prefers not to adjust or complete an artwork after the fact, and enjoys the sense of immediacy that is conveyed by drawing on site. Working in pencil, ball point pen, and Japanese sumi brush, he tries to convey "the spirit of the concert, that ineffable nature of a great performance."

The Norman Rockwell Museum is honored to present the artist's original drawings and sketchbooks, along with the creatively-designed large scale prints that reflect his enthusiastic love of color, graphic art, and digital technology.

Laurie Norton Moffatt, Director/CEO
Stephanie Haboush Plunkett, Deputy Director/Chief Curator

Norman Rockwell Museum
Stockbridge, Massachusetts

Introduction

I began drawing in my father's hand laundry on the Lower East Side of New York City. He seemed to have an unlimited supply of shirt cardboards that I could use to draw on. Here I am drawing on a stool at the counter while my father is marking laundry and my mother is either ironing shirts or at the Singer sewing machine.

Here I am helping my father stretch curtains on the curtain stretcher.

My job at the laundry was to deliver the wet wash bundles to the sixth floor tenaments where they were hung on lines to dry.

I attended the High School of Music and Art and then studied at Brooklyn College with most of the New York School of Painting, i.e. Mark Rothko, Cliyfford Still, Ad Reinhardt, Jimmy Ernst, et al.

I also studied drawing with the great anatomist Robert Beverly Hale at the Art Students League. Here is where I sharpened my skills in drawing the figure. I have worked in oils, watercolor, lithography, etching and all drawing media.

I set this aside for about 35 years to support my family as a teacher, general contractor and as the Director and Founder of Options, a non-profit educational and career counseling service that has sent thousands of young men and women into productive careers.

I returned to drawing and painting when I retired in the Berkshires where I could be close to the music, theatre and art that I love. Joel Smirnoff, the first violin of the Juilliard String Quartet, caught me drawing and urged me to produce a book for Tanglewood.

In the introduction to my book "Drawing Music" Joel wrote, "As performers, we as artists are ever grateful that Sol Schwartz has helped our expression linger in the air yet a moment longer. We celebrate him for his work and for his musicality."

To my complete surprise, here I am, my work on exhibit at the Norman Rockwell Museum while I'm still alive.

Schwartz

Bill Finn, Composer and lyricist of The Putnam County Spelling Bee and March of the Falsettos.

I would like to thank my son David and my daughter Risa, for all of the help, support and encouragement they have given me in creating this book.

Audience

Very often I'm struck by some of the people sitting around me. Sometimes I just can't see the performers because I don't have an advantageous seat. So, I have included a few of the many drawings I've done of the audience. These drawings have been done on the program, scraps of paper and even paper plates. T
he audience is an essential ingredient in the performance,
and you can see the pleasure in their expressions.

"Sol Schwartz created this elegant profile of fellow aficionado, Harold Mantell(right) So taken with the drawing were Mantell and his family that they requested to purchase the original, but Schwartz prefers not to sell his art. Instead, he produced several prints that became treasured keepsakes. A public relations executive and an award-winning documentary filmmaker, Mantell had produced films on a wide range of subjects, from the 1967 New York Yankees to the Nobel Prize-winning poet, Pablo Neruda."

Stephanie Plunkett

Harold Mantell

EDVARD MUNCH, the preeminently renowned Norwegian painter,
transmuted personal and familial trauma into
visual imagery of universal import. Empire sees the fundamental
components of human existence: birth, love, and death. Munch's pri-
mary source of inspiration was his own life history, which was marked
by suffering, illness, and the death of some of his closest
family members. But Munch was also a product of his time, and
the Bohemian community of his native Kristiania (now Oslo)
and his association with the Parisian and Berlin avant-gardes.
His painting became a kind of religious endeavor, for Munch
hoped, he wrote, to help "understand the meaning of
life" and help others gain "a clearer understanding of themselves."
Munch was born in 1863, on a farm outside of Kristiania. His early
work, consisting primarily of family portraits, was inspired by the art of
Norwegian naturalist painters, among them his mentor Christian
Krohg. However, Munch went on to look for more innovative aes-
thetic models, which he found in Paris and then Berlin. In the 1890s and early
1900s, Munch developed his masterwork, The paintings from this
period comprise the first phase of Life, a cycle of pictures that includes
many of his best-known works. The Frieze draws largely on Munch's
personal memories, including the devastating losses of his mother,
Laura Cathrine Bjølstad Munch, and his sister Sophie to consump-
tion, in 1868 and 1877, respectively, as well as his doomed love affair
with Milly Thaulow, a married woman. After several years of travel and
illness, many spent in and out of sanatoriums, Munch returned to
Norway in 1909, where he remained—barring brief trips—for the rest
of his life. He sought solace in his native surroundings, turning to the
Norwegian countryside and its inhabitants as subject matter for his
art. However, he never abandoned his interest in the human psyche,
as evidenced by a late series of penetrating self-portraits. Munch

BIOGRAPHIES

Kyle Abraham began his training at the Civic Light Opera Academy and the Creative and Performing Arts High School in Pittsburgh, Pennsylvania. He continued his dance studies in New York, receiving a BFA from SUNY Purchase and an MFA from NYU Tisch School of the Arts. Mr. Abraham was named one of *Dance Magazine*'s coveted "25 to Watch" in 2009. His choreography has been presented throughout the United States and abroad, most recently at Danspace Project, Dance Theater Workshop, Fall for Dance Festival at New York's City Center, Harlem Stage, Jacob's Pillow, and in Japan, Montreal, and Germany. As a performer, Abraham has worked with acclaimed contemporary dance companies including David Dorfman Dance, Nathan Trice/Rituals, and the Bill T. Jones/Arnie Zane Dance Company. Mr. Abraham was the recipient of a Creative Development Residency at Jacob's Pillow in 2009, where he began making a new work that will receive its world premiere August 11–15 in the Doris Duke Theatre. The Creative Development Residency Program gives exceptional artists the opportunity to create new work, and is supported in part by the Jacob's Pillow Dance Award initiative.

Nina Ananiashvili is originally from Tbilisi, Georgia. She took her first steps in ballet on the ice and became a champion skater. At the age of ten, she began studying at the Vakhtang Chabukiani Choreographic School, followed by the Moscow Choreographic School under the tutorship of Natalia Zolotova. Ms. Ananiashvili rose to fame as a Prima Ballerina of the Bolshoi Ballet, where she danced from 1981 until 2004. She is the only dancer awarded the three most prestigious prizes in dance: the Gold Medal at the International Ballet Competition in Varna; the Grand Prix at the Moscow International Competition; and the Grand Prix at the USA International Competition in Jackson, Mississippi. Ms. Ananiashvili has performed the most famous roles of ballet on the most prestigious stages around the world since 1988. She has performed with the New York City Ballet and, from 1993 to 2009, was a Prima Ballerina with the American Ballet Theatre. Ms. Ananiashvili is the first ballerina to be awarded the Russian national prize "Triumph" for the achievements in the field of art. In 2002 she was awarded the prestigious Dance Magazine Award and was selected as a United Nations National Goodwill Ambassador in 2007, for achieving the millennium development goals in Georgia.

Karole Armitage is the Artistic Director of the New York-based Armitage Gone! Dance Company. She was invited by Jacob's Pillow to create a world premiere for the 2010 Season Opening Gala. After dancing in George Balanchine's Geneva Ballet (1973–1975) and with the Merce Cunningham Dance Company (1976–1981), she developed her own unique choreographic style. In Italy, Ms. Armitage served as director of the Ballet of Florence (1996–2000); the Venice Biennale of Contemporary Dance (2004); and was the resident choreographer for the Ballet de Lorraine in France (2000–2005). She has contributed to the repertoires of major dance companies throughout Europe and North America. Ms. Armitage is known for her collaborations with important contemporary artists such as David Salle, she directs opera, and has worked with Spike Lee, Madonna, and Michael Jackson. She was nominated for a 2009 Tony Award for her choreography for the Broadway production of *Hair* and received France's most prestigious award, *Commandeur dans L'ordre des Arts et des Lettres*. Her company performs a new work, *Three Theories*, July 14–18 in the Ted Shawn Theatre.

Monica Bill Barnes founded Monica Bill Barnes & Company to celebrate individuality, humor and the innate theatricality of everyday life. The company is based in New York and has been presented at Danspace Project, Symphony Space, 92nd Street Y, Here Arts NYC, Fall for Dance at New York City Center, and in many cities throughout the US. Ms. Barnes has created twelve evening-length dance works, numerous site-specific events and several cabaret numbers for her company. In addition, the company creates dances outside of the city

David Bakalar

© Sol Schwartz

Arthur Collins

Sol Schwartz

Jasha Levi

© Sol Schwartz

Lou Steinberg

Jeffrey Borack

© Sol Schwartz

Sol Schwartz

John Hirsch

Dennis Nolan

Theatre

My work in the theatre started at Shakespeare
& Company many years ago. Tina Packer is the
founder and creator of Shakespeare & Company.
Here she is reading a few lines from
Romeo & Juliet in her magical way.

What follows are drawings done when Shakespeare
was at The Mount, of "A Midsummer Night's Dream"
with Tina's son Jason Asprey, Tod Randolph, Jonathan
Epstein as Bottom, Allyn Burrows as Oberon. These
were done in the dark, at night, outdoors, in the woods.

The drawings of King Lear were done at the
Founders' Theatre with Jonathan Epstein as
King Lear and Jason Asprey as Edgar.

The last set of Mengelberg & Mahler posters were
done at the new Elayne P. Bernstein Theatre.
They show the author Daniel Klein and the star
Robert Lohbauer. These were all done in the dark.

A Midsummer Night's Dream

Oberon

Titania

Puck

Bottom

Shakespeare & Company

King Lear

"A powerful lord in King Lear's court, Gloucester is one of the old guard. The struggle following Lear's retirement pits Gloucester against the younger generation. After he is blinded, he finally gains insight into who his children really are. Vividly captured in Schwartz's art, this dramatic portrayal features Johnny Lee Davenport as Gloucester in King Lear, performed at Shakespeare & Company in 2003."

Stephanie Plunkett

King Lear

Shakespeare and Co presents.

Mengelberg and Mahler

Schwartz

© Sol Schwartz

Robert Lohbauer

Elayne Bernstein Theater

Shakespeare and Co presents.

Mengelberg and Mahler

Daniel Klein

Elayne Bernstein Theater

Sweeney Todd

Sketches for the Barrington Stage, Sweeney Todd production were all done in the dark. The following two pages show the original sketches and how they were developed in color for Barrington Stage Co. posters.

Drawings for Absurd Person Singular were done during rehearsal and in the light at the Barrington Stage Co. You can see the difference in the detail in the drawing of Christopher Innvar, when I can actually see.

Sweeney Todd

The Demon Barber

© Sol Schwartz

Christopher Innvar

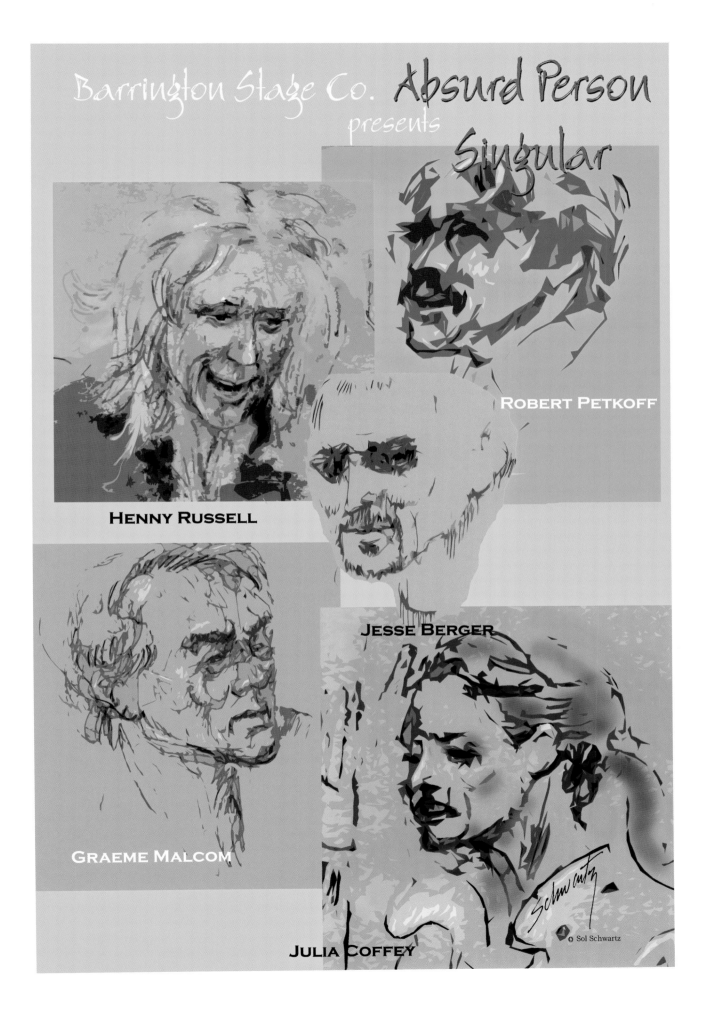

Pillow Notes

by Maura Keefe

The PillowNotes series comprises essays commissioned from our Scholars-in-Residence to provide audiences with a broader context for viewing dance.

In 1992, Mark Morris's dancers crawled out the wings of the stage at the Manhattan Center Grand Ballroom. Mark Morris Dance Group was back in the United States after three years as the resident company of the Théâtre Royal de la Monnaie in Brussels, Belgium. Michael Feldman was there, conducting the Orchestra of Saint Luke's and the singers of the New York Virtuoso Singers. A lot of critics were there; ready to witness the new maturity of the artist who had been in exile and in ecstasy in Europe. And there was a large audience of dance lovers and Morris fans. It was an unusual theatre for a major company to perform in, as audience members climbed several flights of stairs to enter the lushly appointed ballroom. The organization of the undertaking, the sheer number of performers, and the anticipation of the event, caused a frisson in the air. And Morris delivered.

To the magnificent sound of Antonio Vivaldi's "Gloria in D," the dancers crawled, rose to their feet, lifted themselves slightly higher by linking their fingers between their legs and then returned to the floor. In a gloriously awkward manner, the dancers seem to evolve and yet feel no remorse about returning to the crawl in the primordial ooze. This was not the first time the dancers had performed *Gloria*. It premiered in 1981, and was revised in 1984. Nor would it be the last time it was performed; in fact, for a long time it was considered Morris's signature work. Rather, this episode of dancers crawling, standing, lifting, and crawling again serves as a metaphor. This one moment in the performance, that one day in April, can be seen as a part that sums up the whole. This section of the dance, like Morris's choreography at large, is at once unwieldy and graceful, sacred and profane, reverent and repellent. In this movement phrase, as in so many of Mark Morris's dances, the dancers launch from and are bound to the earth, in a beautiful struggle explicitly and profoundly human. Morris's choreography nourishes and sustains us, just as it startles, antagonizes, and steals our breath.

When Mark Morris choreographed *Gloria*, he displayed his rich understanding of structure—both musical and choreographic, his sense of movement invention, and a demonstration of the beauty that can be displayed in form. This dance served notice, foreshadowing dances to come like *L'Allegro, il Penseroso ed il Moderato* (1988), *Mosaic and United* (1993), and *V* (2001).

For a long time, Morris's charismatic off-stage personality and bold dance works led dance writers to refer to him as "the bad boy of modern dance." These days, Morris is no less relentless in his assertive presence, both on and off the stage, but audiences and critics alike have recognized that this man's intelligence and corporeality are anything but boyish. This imagined fertile soil in which the dancers toiled during that brief season in the Grand Ballroom represents the richness of choreographic investigation that continues to imbue Morris's work.

Morris himself began dancing after being inspired by a José Greco performance at the age of eight. After studying Spanish dance and ballet, he joined the Koleda Folk Ensemble, a Balkan folk dance group. Trace elements of the work of early modern dance pioneers and folk dance styles appear in some of Morris's works, demonstrating a respect for tradition and a concern with form. In certain pieces like *Grand Duo* (1993) and *The Office* (1994), the influence of the Balkan folk dancing is apparent in the floor patterns and rhythmic footwork.

Dance

In the woods, in Becket is the World center for dance. Every summer Jacob's Pillow hosts the greatest dancers and choreographers, and I have been privileged to see them and draw them.

I will often draw on a program and because it is usually pitch black I don't get to see the drawing until the lights go on, like the one on the left.

Dancers don't sit still. They are usually flying through the air and it is a trick to try and catch them in motion as you will see in the following drawings from Jacob's Pillow.

Because the action is so swift I simply look at the dancers and let my hand go. It catches them almost automatically. High speed drawing in the dark is a challenge, but a lot of fun when it works.

What follows are drawings of individual dancers, choreographers and their companies.

Baryshnikov

Bill T. Jones
Dancers

To Sol,
Thank you!
Bill T. Jones
7/02

Bill T. Jones

Jacob's Pillow

Let's Dance!

Cloud Gate

These dancers from Taiwan pushed 3 tons of sand around on the stage as they danced and built a fire in a bowl.

The figure on the right had a large pole and brush which he used to push the sand around as if he were father time.

These drawings were done with a Japanese brush in the dark.

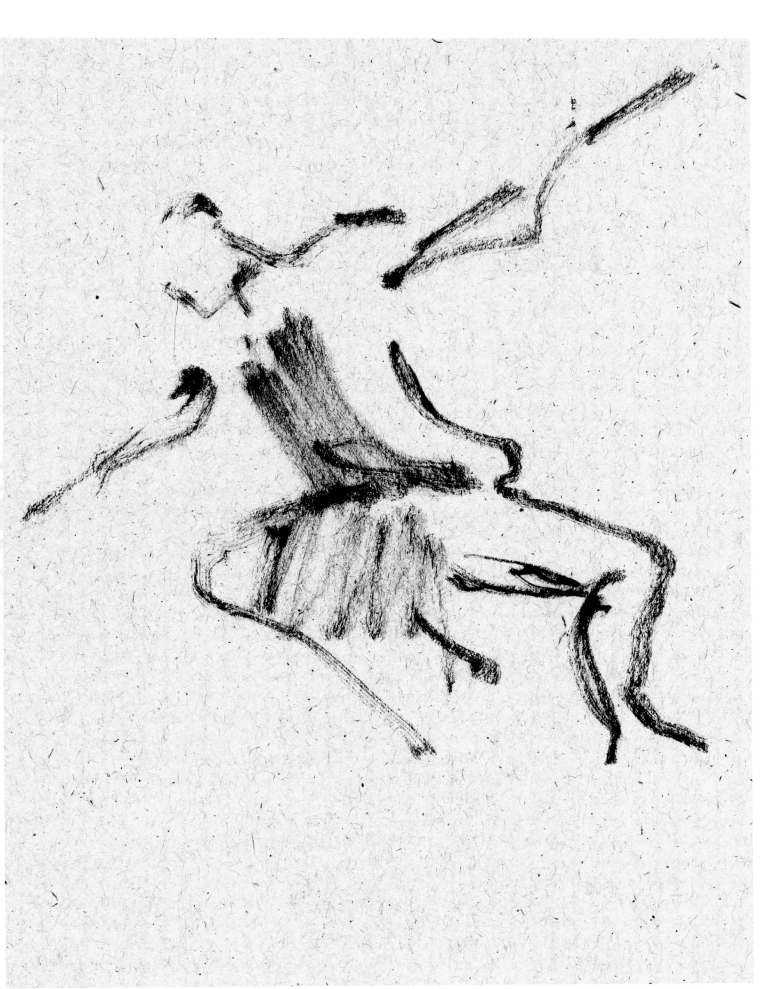

Katherine Dunham

93rd Birthday Party honoring the great dancer
and choreographer Katherine Dunham

She sat on stage viewing all of her dance
protégés performing her work.

Savion
Glover

Savion Glover danced
for Katherine Dunham
at her party.

Schwentz

"The buoyant, fluid style of tap legend
Savion Glover is reflected in this drawing,
which was done with ink and brush
during the dancer's performance at Jacob's
Pillow. Low light is not an impediment for
Schwartz's work, as he rarely looks down
at his paper while sketching on location.
His marks are created in response to the
rhythm and movement of his subjects."

Stephanie Plunkett

Hubbard Street

Nacho Duato

Gabriel Blanco

gabsgabi@hotmail.com

7.23.03
NACHO DUATO
CND2 at the Pier

Nuria Pomares Rojas

Maria Pages

MARIA PAGES at JACOBS PILLOW   JUNE 25, 2003

With all
my love for
SOL
Angel Muñoz

Orbo Novo
Drawn in the dark

"This lyrical abstraction was inspired by a performance of Orbo Novo, a dance created by Belgian-born choreographer Sidi Larbi, and premiered by the Cedar Lake Contemporary Ballet at Jacob's Pillow Dance Festival in July 2009. The piece drew inspiration from My Stroke of Insight, a memoir by Dr. Jill Bolte Taylor, who chronicled the scientific study of her own stroke.

Created on site at Jacob's Pillow Dance Festival in Becket, Massachusetts, these painterly drawings convey a strong sense of movement, created in near darkness with ink and a brush."

Stephanie Plunkett

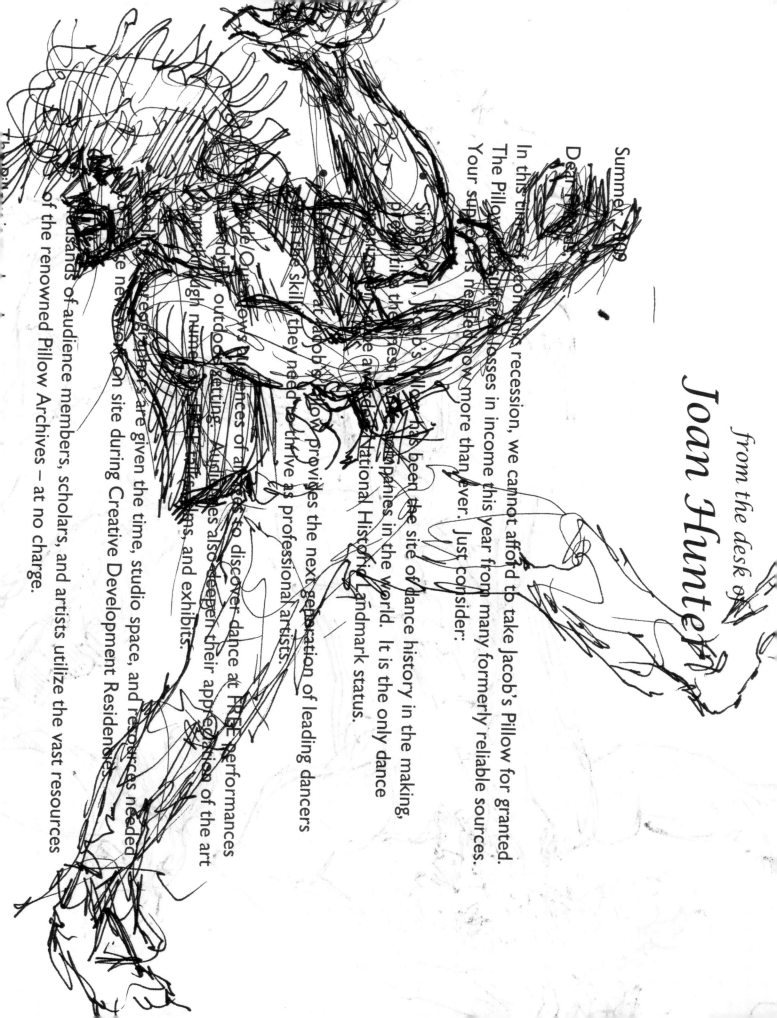

from the desk of

Joan Hunter

Summer 2009

Dear [...]:

In this time of [...] recession, we cannot afford to take Jacob's Pillow for granted. The Pillow [...] losses in income this year from many formerly reliable sources. Your support is needed now more than ever. Just consider:

[...] Jacob's Pillow has been the site of dance history in the making, [...] the [...] companies in the world. It is the only dance [...] National Historic Landmark status.

[...] the skills they need to thrive as professional artists.

[...] Pillow provides the next generation of leading dancers

[...] audiences of all ages to discover dance at FREE performances

[...] outdoor setting. Audiences also deepen their appreciation of the art

[...] through numerous Talks, Pillow Talks, and exhibits.

[...] others are given the time, studio space, and resources needed

[...] are new works on site during Creative Development Residencies.

[...] thousands of audience members, scholars, and artists utilize the vast resources of the renowned Pillow Archives — at no charge.

Rennie
Harris
and Dancers

Schwartz

Peace to you
Harris

Paul Taylor
Dancers
Petrushka

Twyla Tharp

Schwartz

Yo-Yo Ma

Tang

nd Mark Morris

ewood

YO-YO MA and MARK MORRIS DANCERS
CELLO SUITE No. 3   J.S.BACH
OZAWA HALL   JUNE 30, 2003

Music

I started my career as an illustrator at the Tanglewood Music Center.
I kept a diary of drawings of all the artists I saw. Sometimes
on the programs, sometimes in sketchbooks. Someone at Tanglewood
caught me at it and asked me if I would do a book for them
and that was my first book called "Drawing Music."

Since this is a place that hosts the greatest
musicians in the world and the students who
study with them, it was my great privilege to be
able to sit in on rehearsal and capture a sense
of their music when they performed.

What follows is a selection of drawings
done over a 10 year period. The drawing
on the left is of Ann Hobson Pilot done
10 years ago and Kurt Masur
on the right done last year.

The drawings are divided into the
following categories: guest artists,
conductors, Boston Symphony
Orchestra members and
Tanglewood Music Center
students and teachers.

Guest Artists

Garrick Ohlsson

Tanglewood

Garrick Ohlsson

Garrick Ohlsson gave an all Chopin recital at
Ozawa Hall. His playing was brilliant.

I have come to realize that the better the playing, the better my drawing.
They seem to go together. The advantage for me at Ozawa hall, unlike
Jacob's Pillow and the theatre, it is not pitch black, I can see a little bit.

The drawing on the following page, done with a
Japanese brush catches the beauty of his performance,
his likeness and his hands in action. He loved it.

The poster on the left I drew on the program donors page
which Tanglewood liked because in the background there were many
of the important donors that support this wonderful institution.

GARRICK OHLSSON OZAWA HALL

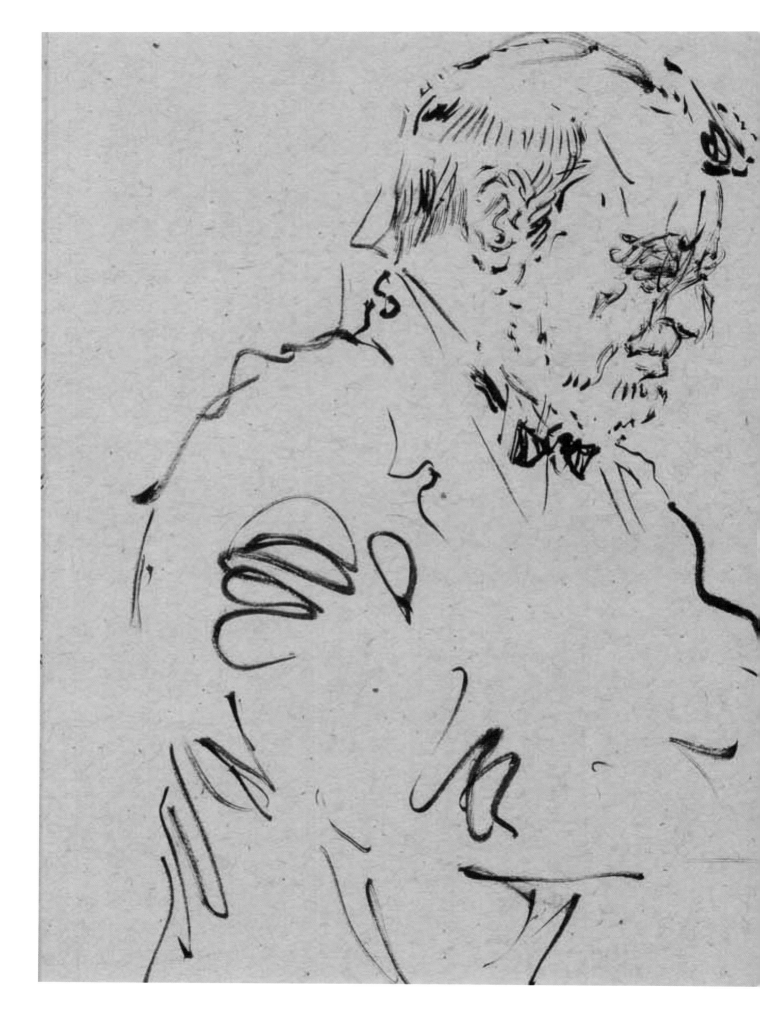

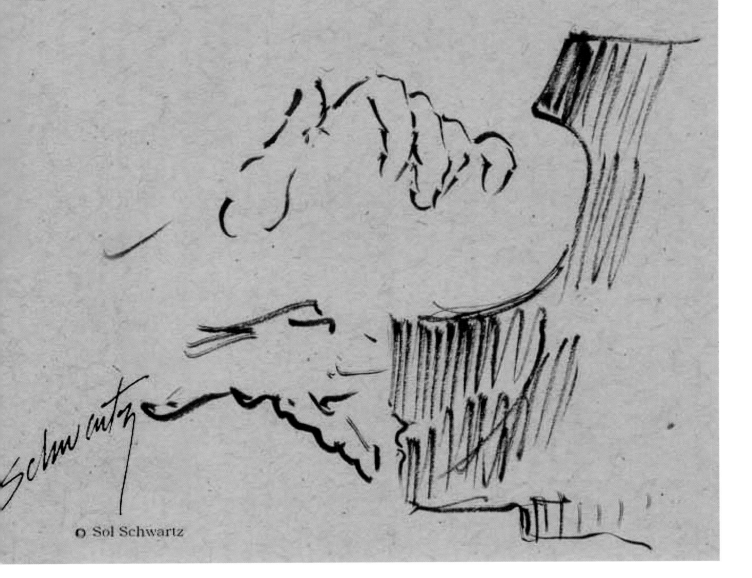

Andre Previn
at Ozawa Hall

PREVIN & FINCK
7·26·98

BRYN TERFEL 8.98

'Tangle Itzhak Perlman

"A child prodigy, Israeli-American violinist Gil Shaham debuted with the Jerusalem Symphony Orchestra at just ten years of age. Since then, he has performed with many of the world's leading orchestras."

Stephanie Plunkett

Schwartz
SHAHAM

Tognetti

Australian

Baltrop

© Sol Schwartz

Chamber Orchestra

Malcolm Lowe joined the Boston Symphony Orchestra as concertmaster in 1984, becoming the tenth concertmaster in the orchestra's history, and only its third since 1920. He is captured here performing a challenging and emotional violin Sonata by Richard Strauss, which he presented with pianist Emanuel Ax.

Schwartz

7.23.99
EMANUEL AX

David Finkel

Phillip Setzer

Emerson String Quartet

Yo-YoMa

Yo-YoMa rehearsing the
Haydn Cello Concerto

To Sol,
Best Wishes
Sandy Koufax

Schwartz

"Sol Schwartz captured the great Russian conductor and violist Yuri Bashmet in this lyrical brush study. "Every seat in Ozawa Hall was taken. I sat on the stage, so my view of Basmet was of his back," the artist recalled of the experience. Bashmet had come to Tanglewood to perform with Emanuel Ax, Malcolm Lowe, and Yo-Yo Ma, in a program that took place during a dramatic thunderstorm that blacked out the auditorium and brought rousing applause because the musicians continued to play in the darkness."

Stephanie Plunkett

Kalichstein
Laredo,
Robinson
Trio

KALICHSTEIN LAREDO TRIO
10.4.98

Dear Sol
I thank you for
this beautiful portrait!
All best —
I am J

To Sol —
Many thanks!

Gagaku

SASSMOTO TAKESHI
• RYUTEKI •

"GAGAKU"
REIGAKUSHA 7/23/96

" GOSHOOROKU no KYOO

Gagaku

"One of the world's senior and most distinguished quartets, the Borodin String Quartet made a rare United States appearance at Tanglewood, a musical experience that Schwartz greatly enjoyed. Close collaborators with Shostakovich in Russia earlier in their career, the ensemble performed his Quartet No. 11 in F minor, Op. 122, and Quartet No. 12 in D-flat, Op. 133. Founding member, cellist Valentin Berlinsky, who died in 2008, is pictured here."

Stephanie Plunkett

Borodin
7.24.03

Peter Serkin and Ozawa

"Always observing the world around him, Sol Schwartz created a likeness of musician Heath Marlow while volunteering at the Koussevitsky House at Tanglewood, and his drawing caught the eye of Joel Smirnoff, first violinist of The Juilliard String Quartet. Little did Smirnoff know that Schwartz had already filled a sketchbook during the quartet's rehearsals at Ozawa Hall. Schwartz's individual drawings of Joel Smirnoff (first violin), Ronald Cope (second violin), Joel Krosnick (cello) and Samuel Rhodes (viola) impressed the ensemble, and were requested for use on the cover of an upcoming CD. Their portraits were assembled digitally, and are seen here from left to right."

Stephanie Plunkett

Juilliard String Quartet

Nelson Friere

STEVEN HOUGH Mozart. 24
James Conlon   7.18.98

Steven Hough

Pieter Wispelway

Performed the six cello suites by Bach at Ozawa Hall.

Pieter Wispelway

Schwartz

© Sol Schwartz

© Sol Schwartz

Sarah Chang

"A diminutive drawing of Tanglewood Music Center Fellow Sarah Chang was enlarged and colored digitally by the artist, to dramatic effect."

Stephanie Plunkett

SARAH CHANG
SIBELIUS.

Kikuei Ikeda

Violist of the Tokyo String Quartet

Michael
Kopelman

First violin

Conductors

LEVINE
at
Tanglewood

© Sol Schwartz

Kurt Masur
at
Tanglewood

Kurt Masur

Kurt Masur autographed this drawing and when he saw the drawing on the left he said "I must have that drawing" and so I sent him the drawing.

© Sol Schwartz

Seiji Ozawa

Charles Dutoit

Tamara Smirnova

Dutoit conducts

Yan Pascal
Tortelier
4.98

Schwartz

John Williams
7.99

CONLON - MAHLER
19.00

James DePriest

"Robert Spano is recognized as one of the brightest and most imaginative conductors of his generation. Now in his tenth season as music director of the Atlanta Symphony Orchestra, he was recently named Music Director-Designate of the Aspen Music Festival and School, where he will assume the title of Music Director in 2012."

Stephanie Plunkett

Robert Spano

"LECTURE ON NOTHING"
by CAGE

Robert Spano

Raphael Fruhbeck de Burgos

8·26·98
Rostropovich

Lucia
Liu

Boston Symphony Orchestra Members

Ed
Barker

Malcolm Lowe
7.12.03

MARTHA BABLOCK.

BURTON PINE
8-18-00

KESUKE WAKAO
OBOE
6.14.98
BEETHOVEN
VARIATIONS INC

MARK McEWEN
OBOE

ROBERT SHEENA—ENGLISH HORN

Ozawa Rehearsal

In loving memory MaryLou Speaker Churchill,
Principal Second Violin

Eskind Zaretsky Trio

Миша Тарельник

Tanglewood Mu

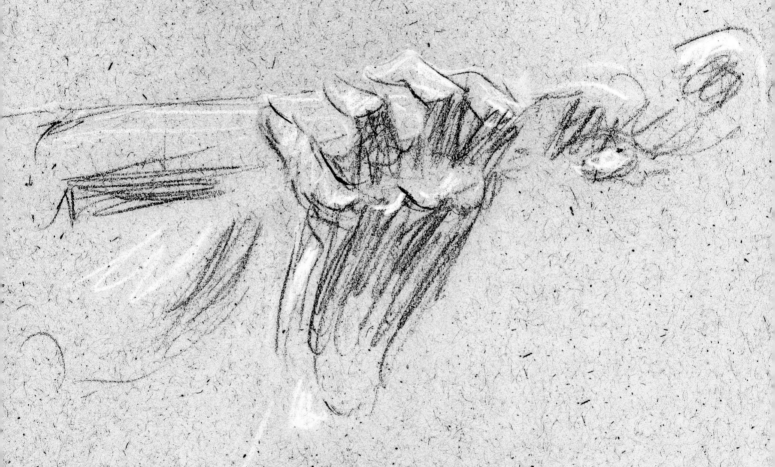

ic Center

Joel Smirnoff performing
with a TMC String Quartet

Rafeal Popper-Keizer

6.29.99 P.K
RATZ

RAFAEL

8.98

Rostropovich

Rostropovich Master
Drora Kaker Close

T
a
n
g
l
e
w
o
o
d

Jory Fankuchen
Music Center

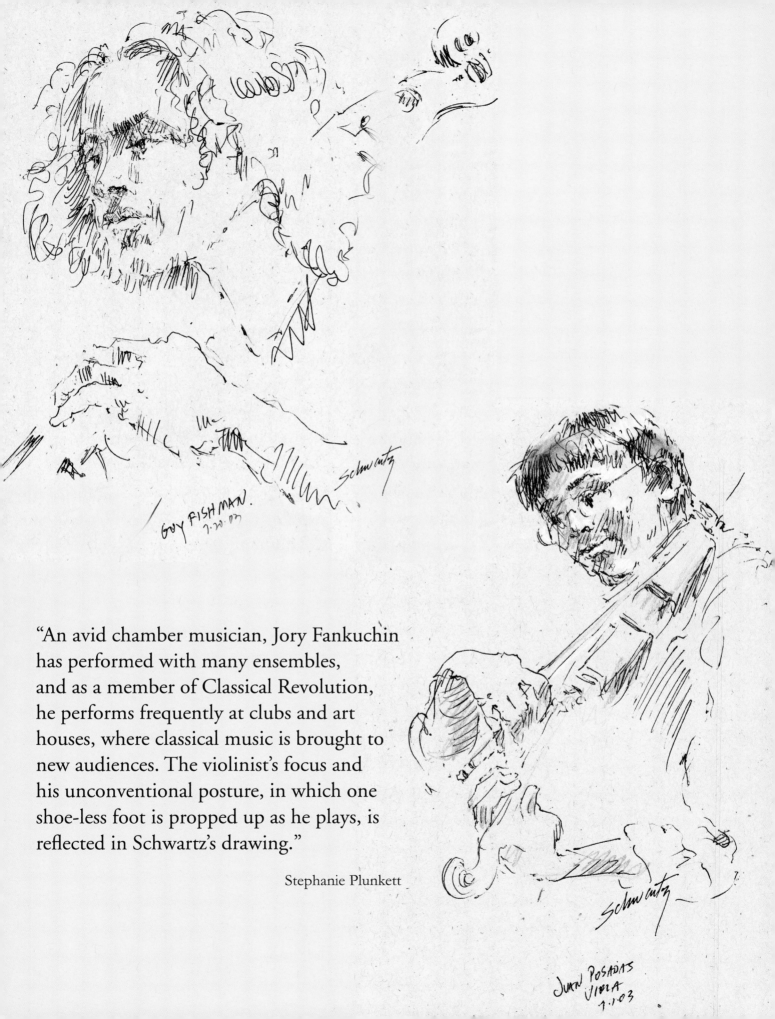

GUY FISHMAN.
7-20-03

Schwartz

"An avid chamber musician, Jory Fankuchin
has performed with many ensembles,
and as a member of Classical Revolution,
he performs frequently at clubs and art
houses, where classical music is brought to
new audiences. The violinist's focus and
his unconventional posture, in which one
shoe-less foot is propped up as he plays, is
reflected in Schwartz's drawing."

Stephanie Plunkett

Schwartz

JUAN POSADAS
VIOLA
7-1-03

BRAHMS TRIO

KINYON a/b TRIO H.29 NICK TZAVARAS

Tanglewood Music Center Bass player

ISBN: 978-1-4507-8734-5 (Hardcover); 978-1-4507-8735-2 (Softcover)

Design and Production
Studio Two, Lenox, MA studiotwo.com